Selective memories

ANA B CASTANO

ISBN
978-1-959314-65-3 (Paperback)
978-1-959314-66-0 (eBook)
978-1-959314-64-6 (Hardcover)

Table of Contents

Personal Thoughts

I'm here 4 years later writing the English version of my first book. Thanks to all the beautiful people that has shown in my life, to stay for a day or 2, for months or for years, all of them Ive welcomed and the lessons I've learned are priceless, the numerous experiences to die for and that's why writing its so fun for me. I'm invite everyone to enjoy the ride of life, no matter what it brings, live your life to the fullest, without expectations and knowing that only the best is happening for you right now. If you keep that thought nothing will bother you again and you'll find the happy ever after in you!

Prologue

At last I found what I was looking for, it cost me a lot of work to find it, it cost me lots of years of my early life, -it cost me a fortune-to discover something that it came with me, born with me, and tons of time to realize a hidden truth that even thought it was acknowledge and conceived by me, sometimes I used to let it go. Perhaps wanted to flight high, like the seagulls, or the Andean Condor-which I found out is the second bird that flights the highest after the Ruppell's, I am from that place, The Andes; no wondering I was so attracted to them just by looking and follow their route till my sight permitted, I was always curious where they go, but they fade with the blue skies and the horizon where I couldn't see nothing more. I wanted to know what was there beyond those places they flew and I couldn't see, always curious about what their eyes would see and what I was missing. I also always attracted to the sun and the moon, and of course the stars, why the shine so spectacular with such a tiny light I was just a kid, a teen exploring the world, a girl who wanted to flight and see more of what it was there. I wondering the ocean and always the blue skies what they have to tell me, I also born surrounded by beautiful palm trees, The Wax Palm, the tallest in the world…no wondering I like to flight high it was my nature. I Remembered those palms how I observed them and become obsessed about their height, their colors the rhythm they have when they dance with others, I saw they born in the valleys and grow to the tallest mountain pic, I saw they were witness of my first kiss, yet innocent and full of passion. Then that man that one day was my husband kept that with him in his memory like I did.

I was born free spirit, I must have music in my words, poetry in my thoughts and craziness all over. I guess I have more of the last and less of the music, I was finding my way to free me no wondering it was always in me but quietly hidden within.

I've lived lots of experiences in a very short amount of time and I do like it, then I realized these are not enough for me, and then life continues surprising me with more experiences, more adventures and more people I get to know. We are here to do something, to shine our light, perhaps to light the way to others, perhaps just to be here and live this beautiful experiences we call life, for sure to do more, to inspire, to help to love…to share the lessons learned. I always share what I know but found out that some people are so protective of what they know thinking nobody else could know…because of those I feel motivated to tell more, so I learned that pride without humbleness wont serve but deprive, power without knowledge of the journey is dangerous and all of this feelings of anger, loneliness, hate and despair are only thoughts that can be jus earned when we are ready to live more and be happy and content with ourselves.

Very close to me nowadays I experienced from people that are close to me these situations that made me realized the source of their unhappiness and make me strong to face the beautiful reality that I got to learn while going out and flight hight. The concept is very simple, but as they rae simple concepts, people don't pay that much attention to it, happens is within us, love is us and by honoring ourselves and becoming in love with ourselves we find the happily ever after goal.

My thoughts lately are focus on how to transmit to people that what they are looking for is just inside us, within us, people survived without the luxury of living which is kept in their minds as they like to reply memories from the past that don't serve anymore, and they are just the past, painful as they might be they don't even exists anymore, so if the memories are to reply let the most beautiful and memorable ones be the protagonist on our daily thoughts.

Introduction

I wasn't born in an average home, and I say-average home-as the one is structured with the parents and siblings. Mi mom divorced my father while I still in her womb, I grew up with my grandparents and I saw my mother very occasionally, when my grandma died I was already 6 years old and then I moved with my mom. I still recall the funeral of my grandma, she was young and I knew I wouldn't see her again, I think is the longest Ive cried in my life.

My first memories as a child go back to an afternoon resting on my aunt's lap, She was looking for lice in my head which she was annihilating at a rate of 50 cents each-if you don't pay I wont allow you to touch me-I told my aunt while she affectionately nodded so she could pamper me.

My aunt used to live next door of my grandma, so all my cousins said That I was the preferred grandchild and niece of my grand ma and aunt respectively, that put me in a lot of trouble with my cousins. One of my cousins also used to live next door to my grandma, and we used to play together outdoors all the time, as soon as we came back from school, we played hopscotch all the time, it was endless, we couldn't stop even to go to the bathroom, we hold for a while till some grown up commanded us to g, otherwise they wont allow us to play more.

My cousin Esther was tough, she enjoyed with me while playing and busy but I knew she didn't like me much as every opportunity she had she will punch me or pinch me if no one was around, and that was cause everybody was giving me more attention than to the others my age in the family. My mom protected her a lot, so we always got the same toys from her in different colors, we play housekeepers and had tea in our tea sets, but if hers broken or disappear mine was always the replacement. We got both in trouble as we used to cut the flowers out the bushes that were in the neighborhood, we used either to decorate our nails or to put flowers in our heads, those are happy memories, and all I recall form those times with her are the fun we both used to have. We of course still see each other and we recall those beautiful memories to celebrate our roots and friendship. In all honesty the pinches and the punches never bothered me and today while writing them I just laugh, it was her way to express her frustration towards the attention I got and the lack of it she had.

Esther used to have a lot of troubles with my grandma, every pinch I had i always told my grandma I never kept to myself any wrongdoing of someone towards me, and either my grandma or my aunt were my shield, after that always happy camper and actions happened, then were part of the past and every new day I was good as new…still continue living that way. I never hold grudges with others, that never will do good to ourselves, our body nor our mind and soul, whatever happens today it needs to be care today, so our life continue healthy and sane.

The child routine started with my grandma, handing me money from the bottom drawer of a tall chest as my daily allowance for school, from which all those monies will be spending in all kind of candies. I liked the monies, and since I recall I was a negotiator with every member of my family. I understood very early in life that monies gets you things you like and entertain you, so I became friends with money, early in life and that have served me well.

Now it was time to eat…

Eating for me like for the majority of people is a very important pleasure, and the memories of food started with my grandma, every Friday night she was baking a cake, and I was the helper the sub chef. The smell of nutmeg is in my head and nose since then, I think I add nutmeg and cinnamon to every meal, and I love it, perhaps it was the kind of experience that it made me have a sweet tooth…The texture of the dough was so silky the color was shiny and the taste…to dye for. I loved Friday nights baking with my grandma. Next morning she used to take me to church, she walk with me holding my hand all the time, all that route to the church and coming by my only thought was to eat the cake, and every stop for me was torture, but I knew that we have to be home before lunch time so I was happy anyway and eating cake for dessert or while any family celebration was a huge thing for me, I think that's why I do like to entertain so much, those happy memories of gathering around a meal makes you who we are now and of course who you want to be. Memories that shape your life, only allow those great ones and beautiful to shape you. Anyway as all beautiful stories and periods of life this child memories end with a very eventful fact, it was shocking and also marked a milestone in my life.

My mom came on a regular morning as my grandma was taken to the hospital the night before, she dresses me up and I was up to go, the yellow dress was short and I love it cause I like my legs and they were exposed, I didn't know which way we were going but I was kind of excited to find out. We stopped at the cemetery, the only one in town, and I saw this heavy coffin carried by 4 people I know, all of them were my uncles, and I dint know what was going on, till I realized it was my grandma in there… it was the day that I've had shed more tears in my life, I didnt want to accept the fact she wont be with me no more It was 2 weeks before my 6 birthday and perhaps the thought of not having my cake bothers me even more. I remembered that day like yesterday, but when I think about my grandma is one the good memories she shared with me and that day was just a closing time for what I could have with her, I guest she is one of my angels, perhaps she is my daughter now, she is around I feel her all the time, but as hard it is to lost someone I think is more beautiful to think of them with the experiences you had.

CHAPTER 1

Committed to Love

3 decades ago i was at the balcony of my mothers house looking at the sky at night and contemplating the stars while writing a poem I am about to share here. even as a child I understood that life is more than a daily routine, a time share with family and friends, I knew it was more and I dint know I was in that search of finding myself as a teen…

The stars and the moon live in the sky…
what is behind that moon and stars that
every night they don't stop to shine?

It was 2003, 15 years after at the balcony of my empty place surrounded by palm trees and feeling the breeze of the winter time in Miami, at the same time perhaps I looked at the skies and found the same moon and same stars and I asked them why was I feeling so lonely.

Asylum in a country who had given me so much, but away from the people I've always loved-my family- I think is a hard situation for someone who always wanted to cheer love and goodness with everyone.

It took me couple of years to leave my country to start a new life, I was divorced with a little child and prosecuted for some guerrilla group that didn't allow me to work at peace. I had a life in a place I knew, in a place I grew up, but from one day to the other all was changed and then I realized another big moment in time started for me, so I decided to be hopeful and start setting a new start, and of course healing from a past I will call was rough for me. So again started to erase some memories that wasn't good and clean the thoughts with the only ones who will bring joy and hope, and for the first time understood the concept of selective memories and actually being aware that was the thing I've been doing since I was born in order to survive and continue with my life. I was starting to be shaping by circumstances, men, time and also places…

Man is born good, society corrupts him" Jean Jacques Rousseau

I wanted to say that not to everyone society has that power, some of us revels at heart refuse to fit in the general. That night at the gathering of all my experiences and thoughts I could recall that I wont let my experiences to shape me at their pace, but to make myself strong in my beliefs and to keep my essence at all times.

I would like trough my writings to inspire or perhaps awake that little one inside of you, as the one who is reading this right now that love is the only force who has the power to move us in the right direction, that no matter what happened to us in the past or who did what to us and what have you we don't permit past circumstances to change who we really are. To touch a heart will be already a win, and for you to understand that Love is the root of everything and it's all we need to live consciously happy and in rhythm with nature will be the greatest success someone can achieve, If you let passion to move you and love your inspiration it will be your happily ever after story with you.

Love is the greatest thing on earth, I love all cubans that go around with the phrase in their tongue, and all the wisdom is in it true love move mountains and clean desperate thoughts, and it makes real of those dreams we have even those of become multimillionaires!

The infinity love is grateful for sunny days and also for the rainy and grey ones, as it understood that contrast is needed, Do not complain for things that could and didn't happen, all stories and experiences of our lives have taken us to the place we are now and it has the value right there, the lessons we learned, the place we have been, the now, if you can be grateful for all the experiences life has taken you and continue to move forward to a place you want to be, it will just happen and you have to be certain that all is happening for the highest it can happen to you! Be grateful and all fall into place.

CHAPTER 2

LOVE

It is like the moon and it is like Mr. Sun
far away from you but it feeds you and give you warmth
You never can touch it, but you know where it is
because your lips can feel it although
they don't kiss you physically
You really know that you have it
that your heart is in peace
here and there and everywhere tell me
boy where have you gone…

Love is enjoy the sun when is at its glare, is to admire the deepest blues of the seas and marveling with the immensity of the firmament. Is to let the feeling of the breeze move you as he is dancing with the trees that surrounds it. Love is to observe the brightness of the greens that in the abundance of their leaves those trees offer us in all their variety. It is to dream about the awesomeness of the beauty, is anxious for getting to know it but it's also so quiet and calm, it is impulsive because it makes you to speak your mind, is crazy and impassioned, but it keeps you calm, it takes you to the highest fire but it splash you with the most refreshing waters, it is certainly the most gorgeous thing love is the maximum expression. Love will sicken you'd it will take everything from you, and then you feel full. Love could be sacrifices, a dream, ant at the same time is so real.

It is a coward and Brave at the same time, love are the two ends. It is a light that continues to shine in perpetuity. The fire that starts and the water that refreshes. The love is the perfection the simplicity of the one end and the other that just merged into one.

When you really love you feel so sure and calm, love don't fear nor is in a rush, you feel trusted, it seems like you have the control, the power to flight its wonderful like the truth.

However some people will make love as an excuse of things that happened to them no knowing that every action makes a reaction. Out of all things in life is love or the absence of it that make all the events in the world, we excuse liars because of love, but they also lie because of the lack of it, those who judge and kill excused themselves as they did and were moved by love, but it was actually the lack of it who made the evil in them, it is the fulfillment or the emptiness. Love has one purpose only, the discovery of the truth, however evil people use it as shield others les evil try to buy it and some less guilty prefer to ignore it.

And here I am, totally naked to myself with all this new life in front of me and I am happy, immensely happy with so much eager to continue living!

CHAPTER 3

Living in exile

The decision to leave my country took me about a year, 365 days and each one of its nights. I was living in a constant paradox, that the only thing I could achieved was to destabilize myself. I ended up a part of my life that I felt I left with a negative balance, and an account to my credit. I lived a beautiful life, quiet and in comfort, I was in the search of someone to live with and share my happiness while enjoying the growth of my only child.

In the searching for love the task was little unsuccessful, so I shifted to my professional career, it has been my shield, my retreat and one of my passions, among all I specially enjoy social work, at least I used to-things change-I recall working with the Colombian architect society-kind of the AIA for Colombians, I volunteer myself with them as a prosecutor and everyday with them my commitment to that institution growth to an out of control touch. The same passion who drove to volunteer and give my help to others took me to dark sides and adventures I couldn't imagine would exist in a country so dear to my heart. The same passion was transforming slowly but steady to an estate of despair, fear and instability that only the rigors of a country in war could offer.

Plan Colombia was a world class project funded with bank world resources and sponsored also by USA in order to exterminate drugs and farms who produces all kind of raw material for drugs production and replace those with social projects, hospitals, freeways, housing schools among others. I was leading the project for the northern neighbor side of my county and my county itself. Lots of projects were done and successfully funded at the time. in my aim and thorough the process never realized the seriousness of the situation and the anger my doings caused to the subversives groups, and anger and suffer That I lived without signing for it. In my thoughts I was only doing good things and contributing to a noble cause, but others saw it as a threat of the freedom of a country that has always been. Perhaps I was so naive to think about the bad things or the bad guys, I was so much like that for a while, now while still being naive I have experiences that had giving me tools to inform me more before to get into something will harm my well being, and following some noble advices that volunteer jobs are not as good as they seem.

Anyhow living in Colombia in the nineties wasn't so appealing, drug lords boomed, violence was the head of the news, kidnappings at a glance and all of decent people were doing were touched somehow by those entities, one night I want out to have dinner with my 3 years old son, and while he was at the playing ground and i was awaiting our food a hitman shoot someone that was sitting less than 250 feels away from us. That shot could hit my son or myself I thought and at that moment I started to learn about fear. I didn't want to live like that, I wont and I didn't sell myself or buy my freedom as a human being.

In my constant personal dialogue I knew that better than that exist, I just didn't know where but for sure exist I said to myself. it has to be a place where life is respected and valuable, where people are kind and good to each other and where good is more noticeable, the noise of the shot guns in my head were bothering me that night but next day was all about a new day, however news on the tv's were reminding me of the statistics of the amount of gun shotted people daily, at some point was unbearable for me to hear in the news "today only 100 people were shut to dead only? I thought…how this heartless humans communicate these news this way? It was a demoralized country and I was living in it, so it was kind of a choice wether to live there and become one of them or go out and find other more civilized ones. I chose the second.

It was a gain for me that in order for my business to exist I had to travel to Miami to get the main source I was selling. I found myself coming to Miami

3-4 times a year for business but great part of those trips was touristing, and getting to know Miami and sometimes shopping, others more fun just lost in the city while traveling in a rent a car. On my way back home I was hoping to see that person who once I dreamed I could have a nice life with.

CA was perhaps a realization of the "don't" do lists, yes is the way I see it. I saw a professional intelligent man that was a little depressed, but with huge potential of being for the both of us, I knew he tried but always the truth at some point comes out. He was a dead man, living in the past, grieving a departure that happened long time ago, we became lovers as we both wanted to be loved, but not him nor I wanted to settle with less than we wanted to. His "want" now was with his friend and I couldn't settle with a man living in the past. As per myself I only wanted to see what I want to see, and made myself a beautiful movie of him in order to pursue that dream I wanted. It happens sometimes that we create images of people that only exists in our heads, and I am now so aware that in the searching of someone I was just getting away. Love is free and is founded at ease isn't complex but we tend to complicate things are not meant for us, perhaps this experience with this dead man was a hint, a call to choose better and to really get to know that person really well and not just making the video we would like to be played

When I noticed how few I had in this place I was born to love or be loved by I started visualizing my life in the land of freedom, my business trips were an important part as I enjoyed them to the fullest and I was so productive and proud of what I was doing.

Every time I landed in my town I had this feelings of emptiness, of this "not the place I want to be", these aren't the people I respect nor admire therefore what is left for me here? that was a constant question spinning in my head, and I knew the answer-my son-,my little one I feel I couldn't protect him really well in a violent and dangerous country in a demoralized country when life was purchased for less than 20 bucks. But that thought came to me that:"perhaps I will open doors for his future.

Within my job, and the volunteer job and a personal life in the making wasn't much for me, people from my job were fun, trustworthy and friendly but they saw me going down on a 180 turn that they started to realize I wasn't there anymore. Everything started to fall down and I just wanted to retreat myself in order to make that decision of starting a new life, was taught, easy to write down than to living it in the moment; but here I am invisible again.

I experienced all kind of emotions at once, I had grudges for all the people didn't understood I was doing good with my volunteer job, I was angry as I couldn't express myself towards the principles were important to me, I was resentful of men weren't ready for me, good thing I was only with myself, letting all those emotions be and go as they appeared and understood at the end of the grieving that once I let all that go I was ready again to start another chapter of my life.

I was surrounded by coffee trees in a land my mom used to have, I remembered I planted lots of flowery trees and by walking those bumpy pathways I also planted underground those emotions I didn't wanted to feel again. I replenish myself with the love and caring and good thoughts I always want to cherish, I was able to heal myself in a record of time as I totally withdraw myself form the world I was saying good bye. I told everyday those coffee trees and pathways about my plans in a different land, they heard me, and they wished me well, without knowing I was making a proper goodbye with the land I call home and the sound of hope in the word I spoke resonate with them and the trees and the paths gave me a farewell too.

I was ready and set to leave I couldn't brought my son with me; then I got one last threat from his dad, perhaps the most deepest one. But I was ready I detoxified my head, my body and my heart and off to go.

I was making sure all the wounds ere closed and healed, I knew it starting a new chapter with new people will take a lot from me, so I better get there soundly great because I did know well that missing my family was the first thought I needed to overcome. My mind was set and so another destiny, another opportunity another try.

CHAPTER 4

Welcome to Miami

"I was born in Miami January 18-2002" That was my answer to an immigration officer at the Miami Downtown Immigration Office, in early March 2002, the day I got granted my application for asylum.

The officer, a woman in her 30's restless and nervous looked at me very surprised, and for a second or two she didn't know what to said to me-as she was corroborating my basic information in the form of an informal interview- and I was speaking in a logical figurative sense. She finally handed the granted asylum documents to me and said "take your papers, here they are your asylum has been approved, you have me very nervous"... She said that as moments ago in the back I was talking to a very narrow audience hopeful and confined in this cold and gloomy room like a prison was contained all of us.

My mouth opened while we were waiting, to talk about the double standards, about love and opportunities, to all of us that like me were waiting for an answer, in that moment I realized that a lot of those people were there landed with a make up story, others while I was listening few moments ago were giving me specific details about the steps to create a good story.

I decided to stop them about all of the nonsense they were talking and like an inspirational speaker my mouth opened and my thoughts came out.

I said to them that the only cases I know were granted for asylum were to those politicians and diplomats from Latin America and other countries while watching the news, However I said I am not a well known politician nor a diplomat, but anyhow if they will reject it I was looking for other countries options, and furthermore another new opportunities will show for me in order to find my freedom. I spoke of the importance of always telling the truth, I said and still abide by that rule that you can't expect much when you lie. All of them looked at me with attention and hope I know but also with a sorrow look and shameless too.

I suddenly heard they were calling my name, as I turned my head I could spot the last two lines of chairs filled with undercover agents who were listening avidly at the stories we were talking and to the words I was saying; they were observing me, and I just starting to fall in love of this place and country while looking with loving eyes to those people were protecting this country.

Then the woman dressed as an officer started to cry like me, with tears of joy, and I had the time to explain myself and let her know that after all what I suffered in my country i just wanted to start a new life, so I called the day I arrived to the US my new day of birth, after all that was the feeling I got when I landed.

I also was surprised when that cold, calculated woman was shedding tears, as moments ago when called my name she just took rudely the documents I was carrying with me, and furthermore was acting so contemptuously with all others people were waiting in the room; and also she made me felt so good when like me she felt my freedom.

Then the nervous of the woman was limited to my early age of barely 3 months.

I observed from the woman, an apparent hardness, and she shown up and make feel to others like it was her forte, every time she opened that door of the waiting room like more of a prison and yield "next". We all there were prisoners sort of speak, I dint appreciate her rudeness and poor manners, and the derogatory way she was treating all of us. It was an act as part of the job she was doing, we were treating poorly as we all were considering all of the same specie of liars, but when they knew me they respected me and treat me decently, that was my first experience with the conceptualization of double standards. That was new for me

I consider double standard an intellectual capacity to change as convenience with the facts given, nevertheless a great tool for intelligence matters and so I knew what was it and became familiar to it since that day.

We are at a constant rate of change, so its okay to stop, think and change to direct us better, skies and clouds change in matters of seconds it is its nature and so we do, we can too. We need to be humble at some situations in our lives however be careful cause in this society we live in; humbleness might be seen as a weakness or stupidity but for those who see it that way we need to dress ourselves with an armor and show up our greatness with prudence and diplomacy that they just don't know.

> ..." *like a dream, too good to be truth, prefer*
> *to keep sleeping, keep it in the memory*
> *and never wake up.*
> *Im afraid if I see you again, this dream in a nightmare*
> *will turn, and then that never can be undone*
> *This unknown reality of separation without*
> *knowing why, I prefer never to get to know*
> *and this what I feel like a beautiful dream will keep.*
> *Today I feel very poor in front of you and before*
> *your richest of love, like a good part of this dream*
> *today I am getting back to my reality*

That was indeed the more romantic poem someone has written to me. This man was my first love here, he knew how to treat a woman, he showed me the city, the places, the ocean, the restaurants and when he wasn't around, the money to go shopping.

He was a dream love.

I was reading this Brian Weiss book-many lives many masters-while waiting at the HRS department office in Miami and expecting to see a plan reviewer so I can get a permit to build a septic tank. Eddie was waiting like me, but since he noticed my presence he couldn't look anywhere else I was fully aware of that.

At the time of leaving he handed me his bc, and he got my number, why not after all anyone can become a client and you never know, I said to myself, I just had business in my head.

The phone ring was loud and echoing at the empty house with only my friend Cathy and I, the 2 stories we were surrounded by were furnished nicely and tidy and tons of natural lights were shining throughout the double height windows at the early afternoon. She said is for you. Eddie is calling you. I said please say I am not here, I think is this guy I met at this office but he looks a bit old I recall saying. Then she saw a sport car convertible driving around by the parking lot and she said to me, you better answer young lady to this guy. He was in the neighborhood cause I also without realizing gave him my address. Anyhow I managed to talk with him compromising myself as I was focus on my doings, they all were confined to a working life and college studies learning to speak the language in the land of freedom.

He insisted, not once but three times maybe more, till I decided to go out and have lunch with him, a pleasant guy, funny and just charm, It wasn't easy not falling for someone that treats you right and care for you, I wasn't thinking, I just let it flow and I think it came out pretty good for 4 months or so. But the reality stroke and he wasn't the man for me, it was just a first stop of a journey I created for me.

Eddie is a successful Miami guy, who retired not so long ago, his fortune based on hard work and trying and error till he gets to the target as he explained to me one time, took him to a comfortable life, his kids were treasures to him and I really admired that devotion of his for them... He taught me that some men like to control with their moneys, that the macho men idea yields and speak loud when you have moneys, for some average women I thought myself and he agreed. He fall in love without knowing what I wanted, he offered me something some women would love to get but It wasn't for me, I remember saying I just want the whole package, and as of today is that I've always wanted the same. he explained to me clear and loud that all I wanted existed, and were there, and as I was listening he started with backpack story. I was avidly listening to him, I liked him and he shared valuable time with me in my early days here in Miami, I respected him and his advise, he was a friend, a good person to be around with.

He said to me, "that man you want is out there, but be aware he will come with a baggage, a backpack, and it will be in your hands to accept it or leave it". Eddie explained to me that the baggage could contain, kids, ex-wives habits and personal issues that I had to discover and accepted if I wanted the happily ever after story. With that thought in my head I remember iI made a list of must have things this person I want will have to have.

I made the list, so Eddie gave me some advice on being selective, I did like that also good things were important to enjoy life, of course boating in Miami, dining out and having fun was also in my head, but also family and a warm home with kids was always in my head.

For the time being of approximately 6 months Eddie was my cabana boy, I enjoyed without regrets all the time and experiences we had, the rides, the boating the dinning and the deep talks we used to have. But he wasn't the men for me, his life was already made and he was looking for just fun, the family thing he already lived and he didn't want that much reality at this time of his life, it was great while it last and so we both accept it to leave it just right there. I was ready for that special one now already with an specific profile, and I was excited and thrilled of the things I learned from him, the places we visited, the word he expressed and always the memories we created, I was thankful for him to show in my life.

We learned every single day if our minds are open, and we are focus on what we want, universe gather for us the components of our wants and present it to us in a way of ease and fun, and it is our job to be prepared to receive it and enjoy it. We learned from the tiny thing our eyes can see, however I see people so away from the now while driving in those expressways we use, the speed, the constant surviving mode most people lives their lives by and their stubbornness resonate with a part of my life that I already left and so I feel compassion for those who are in the level once I used to be; and as part of my journey I expressed gratitude again and accept that I am living a new season in my life and feel victorious once again with all the adventures I had and that was able to enjoy and understand all of those happenings are just part of the journey I create.

In order to love freely and well we must be in love with ourselves, we must first need to work in our weakness and healing all those past experiences we might recall and affect the now to be able to accept, to forgive and to give.

CHAPTER 5

Discovering my fears

Perhaps the biggest fear for me was that feeling that my physical existence could vanished from one moment to the other while I was living in that country of mine. Bullying and threats contributed to fueling that fear, and those subversives groups are trained to do exactly as that.

The early days of my arrival in Miami, were intense. Finding a proper car to drive and start running errands and pursuing my legal documents was the first thing I did once I moved with Cathy, housing issue was resolved thanks to a friend of mine that also was in the searching for love and I didn't classified in his category as I was already divorced and with a child, he was a bachelor looking for someone the same. Enrique was a cool friend and he did all he could to set me here with housing and a decent car to drive. The Commute was about 45 minutes in the morning and 30 minutes in the afternoon, I was driving from Miami Lakes to downtown Miami for almost 2 years. The rides were full of paranoia, I was living here with some fears from the place I was coming from, I felt someone was following me at all times. It was a traumatic event for me the day I got confront it with a head of a subversive group while doing some grocery shopping next to my house back in Armenia, that event marked something in myself and some fear for my life started since then. I was already here but feeling the paranoia they will still followed me. One day it was the afternoon, and I called the police as Cathy wasn't home, two officers came and sat down at the dinner table with me, they listened to me without any anxiety nor pressure, I was anxious and seeing them so cool and calm just made me realized it was just paranoia and going crazy myself, that day stopped the feeling, I adopt their words and finally realized I was already somewhere else.

The fears are a personal job that requires acceptance, strength and lots of inner peace. We all at some point of our lives have had experimented fear, some more than others, in different forms and we are not guilty of having them but we cannot become victims of it either as fear will block us and wont allow to live our lives freely. It is important we take time to heal, to listen our bodies and acknowledge our emotions as part of any other feelings of traumatic experiences we could had. We al are bound to anything exist in this world, the good the bad and the ugly, but our bodies also are designed to endure and overcome challenges.

So that fear I felt I could die ended that day with the officer that talked to me with words of wisdom and calm, I love from him the way he talked to me and I decided I will do as he said and so I did.

Costed me some paranoia but It was only few days while the real cure came along.

Among other fears I might carried then I was releasing them one at a time, till I felt completely cured, It was a journey allowing them to surface and acknowledge they were within me, I felt grate and day by day the feeling of safety here growth and growth till I could live more freely. I thought I was ready to love again so Eddie could know that part of me that was only joy and charm, so I gave him all cause I don't know other ways to be with someone without being 100 percent there.

CHAPTER 6

Abc Architectural Business Company

I remember the name wasn't quite good enough for Eddie, he said there is a lot of names that started with those abbreviations, I didn't care that was the name I chose. Sometimes he was mean but I understand now he was just being hard on me, that was the way he knew so thats the way he thought. Whatever we do is always perfect for the time we created.

I spent lots of nights and days writing what could be this business of mine and what they will represent in my life, I gave birth another creation of mine 7 months after I landed here and it was ready, a whole business plan I layer out while getting started here.

While in college taking english as a second language classes some specific opportunities were presented to me, all of them were paid at 15 usd per hour, I didn't like the money it was not enough for me to be happy working for someone else, so one day I decided I just start my own business and give myself a deserving salary.

ABC was created with the intention of helping other professionals like me that were here but unable to work in their craft, and doing projects as I knew for people with some issues with their properties and county taxes unpaid. I wanted to help and by helping others I was also helping myself. I wasn't ambitious enough with my plan my only aim was to learn and to help it was the first steps of me getting into business here. More than a philanthropist as some people like to call, it was me helping me while serving others. Besides those kind of jobs, local architects didn't want to do, they called "strange" jobs so I was very pleased to help in those areas weren't taking care of.

The business was a great idea, I remember in 2007 after 5 years of my creation all kinds of business booming offering the kind of job I designed, I was happy to see that going as this was the time were living this place and embarking to another new journey with a new family of mine.

To start with the firm I needed a registered architect, it was the time I met Felipe Oruña, a gentleman and old man, who became like my dad and grandad all at once, Felipe was a duke and came from Cuba when the regimen took over that place as well. Perhaps we found each other with similar experiences and we became good friends and partners as well. Felipe taught me all I needed to know to present a set of plans to the different municipalities and get the construction permit in order to make the project a reality. It was a very productive and engaging time, every conversation with Felipe was full of content and enrichment. His vast experiences as an architect, inspector and building official for the city of Coral Gables were taking me to another level in my knowledge and everything was suddenly new to me, another country, another language another rules and another process, It was certainly an amazing time of career growth for me, and all that's to that Duke who saw in me something he dear.

My routine started to get in shape, after some exercise in the morning I was set to start my English as a second language classes, then after 11:00 am I was in my new office starting with 2 small commercial projects I engaged. I had a drafter who came to helped me and he was learning like me this new country, Jamie was helpful and will bring me company with my start up.

Those two projects I got, also were presented to me by another acquaint I met at the city, I guess he liked me and wanted to help, I took the help and left the liking to others. Henry was my advertising department and he brought me clients to do as we need. The business started and I was doing architecture in a different country just 7 months after. During that process of starting the business some very specific and special events happened, I was so assertive and focus of my doings and also living the present moment to the fullest, I needed to be so focus in order to avoid mistakes that will cost me money, I was so careful and all I wanted to do was to be productive and professional with my job. The first project was an extension of a local very well known restaurant that was booming, so I became good friends with the chef, Willy knew how to be kind and gentle by offsetting the greedy and the BS attitude of his 2 partners. All I needed was to talk to Willy about his envision for the extension, basically in a very small space the kitchen became essential and functionality was required, we did our best to deliver to the chef and so we did, after some meeting we delivered a presentation with beautiful renderings and all of them were so impressed and happy they hired us. We delivered the project and henry was pleased we did good with the resources we had at the time. He started getting more and more for me, but it was a little uncomfortable as I really didn't know he was trying to get more form me or he was just a helping hand. He wanted more and I could stop it. After he introduces me to Felipe I was basically seeing Henry very once in a while and he also understood I wasn't interested in anything more than business. I felt sorry to lose a great asset I had but I was mature enough to understand that I don't mix work and pleasure at any cost. The second project was rough with the first gain I also lost a friend and with the second I lost a client but gain so much experience that was available to me to gain savvy in my business.

The house of the insurance adjuster was another Miami-an house with a Florida room entrance, low ceilings and divided by arches living space, kind of mediterranean feel as I was getting to know and became very familiar to it. This guy was very suspicious to me since day one.

He asked if my company was insured, and of course I started to observe his actions and requests in order to understand what he really wanted. Apparently he wanted to extend the Florida room of his house, and so I did. Signing the contract happened fast and all his intentions shown pretty quickly as I started developing his project. He used to approved the initial ideas and we continue the process with the city, once approved with the city he rejected and wanted to see something different. As I was gathering my records I recall 3 sets of drawings previously approved by him, by the city and then rejected again and so I needed to start all over again, of course the act was on purpose, when I didn't meet the delivery date the guy hurried to pay all my fees and then suit me for not meeting the time frame. I was cool I knew exactly what I was doing and was able to present to Felipe's lawyer all supporting documents he was impressed with my effectiveness while showing the file of this client he confidently advised us that we didn't have to even go to the court, that he will present all I we dint have to worry for anything nor returning any monies to this guy, moreover I was allow to write another invoice for the extra job he put us in. I did and we won. The intention of this monkey from day 1 was to make effective and suit my company for double the money I charged so he use his adjuster experiences to scam me. He didn't count with the fact that I smarter him by doing the right thing. What a lesson I learned, I was laughing with Felipe as we both ourselves recall the words and numerous callings in a failed intent to get back some of his monies.

This experience taught me to be careful, but not because of it I will change and trust no one, all of us has to be granted the benefit of the doubt, you certainly can learn to be more careful but you don't judge all for the actions of one.

It was a win the company didn't lose money but the client didn't get his wanting, his evil wanting. I am always so proud of no letting anyone to get his Machiavelli's ways and over do me. I am a woman I was maybe new here and in this environment but I was knowing what I was doing and as such I did, he didn't counted that I was one step ahead of him. He started threatened me and trying negotiating in order to get some money back which I totally diminished by acknowledge him all the numerous times I was working in his project, he was also my neighbor in the office building, and it was agreed with the owner of the building and himself that I better empty the space so we don't get in future troubles. I left with my head up and a better and beautiful building place was already ready for me. I didn't feel any fear not even once, my business is a great shield I proudly carry it, I know my craft and I know some people so fear wasn't never a subject but something was true for sure, I was kind of alone and feeling lonely or perhaps homesick as it was already the weekend of a hectic and victorious week, and when I get home I wasn't feeling that victorious after all, I didn't have someone special to share it but I was happy and hopefully that great things were coming my way.

I stopped by the video rental to get a couple fo movies to watch while studying English I specially remember those two that used to repeat and repeat over and over again till the dialogues became so familiar that I was repeating even before they happened, a fun way of learning for me, learning a new language by doing something fun in the way of it…sounds familiar sounds like me.

It was Monday again, at lunch time Felipe was so relieved that all went well with the law suit and nothing happened even to him or to the company. He was happy and relaxed, and my only words I could speak was…"my dearest Felipe Duke de Oruna, stones are thrown at the tree that bears fruits" he laugh and he agreed and feel some relief that I was a smart young woman doing business with him.

Felipe showed me around Miami, the buildings and codes I needed to learn, He guide me with passion and patience and I also enjoyed the stories he used to tell me twice or three times or whatever times that was he was my friend, my partner and he was taking good care of me, I felt protected. His Alzheimer's condition was advanced and started to get worsen at some point that I have to limit my days with him to twice a week and eventually to take him out as he wasn't able to do any work function and had to stay home. Felipe died while I was living in the Middle East in early March 2011. His memories and teachings are dear to me and always so grateful and lucky to have had met him. Friends are treasures and you care for it with your soul, I could see him in his final days but in my memories he remains as the only partner my company had. RIP Felipe you will always be loved and remember with so much joy.

CHAPTER 7

Discovering my Solitude

I started by filling my afternoons with productive activities that fulfill me, like drawing and painting of the things I see around me, as an expression of the reciprocity I find when connect with nature, also the mornings was English class.

My English teacher used to talk to me a lot, and it was that time when you understand everything but you can'tget back with an answer cause you don't find the perfect words of what you are thinking…it was hilarious looking myself with all the words I wanted to say and none of them came out…learning English was a heck of experience for me, I can fill a book with all of them, gratefully I enjoy making fun of myself so any mistake or miss word was just the turning learning point and endless laughing at anything I was saying.

I decided to get a boyfriend that will only talk to me in Englishso and then as I wish he appears, Sam was from Alexandria, either was English arabic or spanish, and the only common ground was English….

Sam laughed very loud at my English flows, and so he was a heck of a teacher, cause i wanted to get back with a good comeback…it took me some weeks but then I was answering back to him the way I wanted and to my surprise he said to me…"you are not funny anymore" now you are speaking English so I guess was just the sign that we were over…he served the purpose!

Back to school teacher was impressed and we start having more sophisticated conversations, like about the things I draw and the way of I want my paintings to be, its kind of my cool concept in arts, I have this theme of drawing what I see and kind of mark a milestone in my life, so i was drawing the second item of my collection at the time of the conversation but I let her know that I will do 9 themes with 9 pieces each one, she looked at my so surprised and she only answer was "what the heck is wring with you?" what the heck is wrong with her...she didn't know about the number 9?...ugh! so I kept my sophisticated conversation and my art to myself since then...but here that I don't have interlocutor is easy to say and that's why I explained whether you like it or not, I don't give a fuck, it is what i want to do and a way to express myself to the world.

The number 9 resonates with me in so many ways, like any other number and every number will resonate with you, usually follows you, you see them in the car tags, or at tickets and what have you...and its a symbol of patience and tranquility to me...is perhaps the reach of completeness and the ability of perceive everything clear. So my art is based on that number that speak to me

First I painted families, I guess I missed my family back in my country and then it was trees all these glorious Royal Palm Tress that Miami and only Miami has! I painted black and white though because I love the markets technique is easy, sharp and clean and don't like to shade things off...I love the way the appear raw and straight, so markets also are appealing to me.

Then Sam took couple of those paintings and bought me from me and I guess he liked to have something to remember me by and so I sold them.

Then the palm trees was another story but I will catch later with those, for now lets say that I have done circles as the meaning of circle of life and how I see everything as a round and not square, then I was in other countries and draw camels with a M shape perhaps because I was married already while there. I know water and skies are coming next but I'm thinking another technique will express better those ideas for my collection of art.

I was filling my days in the best possible ways of productiveness, fun and inspiration, love and joy were always ingredients, love for life, for being here, glad to be in a different land with so many things to say, explore, live and make memories from.

Summer came with countless of rainy afternoons and floods around me, hot and sticky was the norm and drawing and getting crafts at local suppliers were some of my favorites activities while home, also I remembered watching those movies I do like hundreds of times in order to learn English if I rent one over the weekend I could possible watched 30 times daily till I remembered all the dialogs in it… so that decision of going for something and doing it have been living with me for quite some time and I have to say That I enjoy it pretty much…it keeps you moving and crispy at all times.

Following your greatness and what you really want to do brings you joy and bliss, listen to your heart and thoughts and start baking those ideas you have in mind I guaranteed you it will never fail at the contrary fill your life with so many good things.

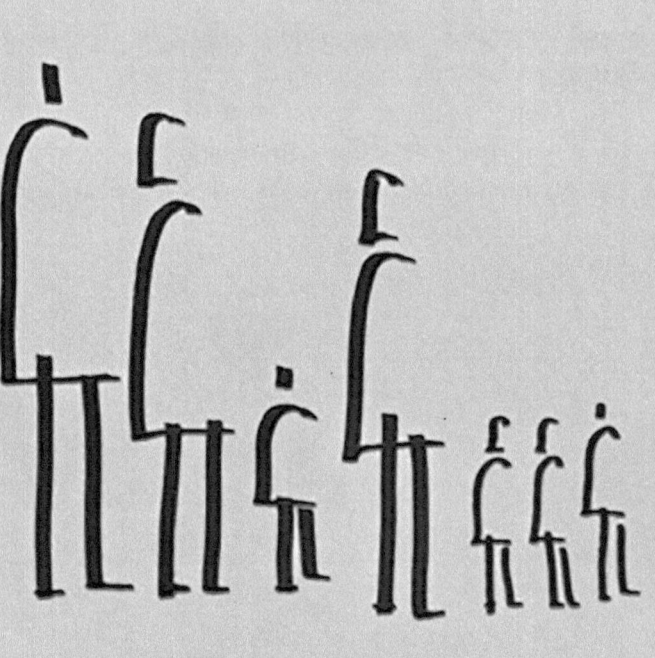

"Familias", marcador en papel de acuarela.

"Palmeras"

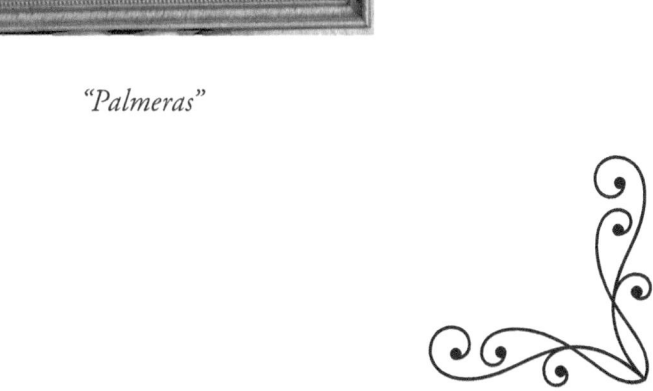

CHAPTER 8

The artist, the neighbor

Ron was about my age, an Italian- American architect that came all the way from the North to work in Miami, -he likes the weather I think like most of the people who come to Florida-. He said hello to me while I was writing in my balcony and he parked his car in front of my townhouse. It was already fall, there were no more rains and weather was a little cooler. The color blue of his car impacted me and call my attention, I never seen such a bright color in a car, -I thought-He got the courage to speak to me, he introduced himself as the neighbor who just happened to live around my block. He was kind, soft and caring, He also is an artist and his technique is oil on canvas, and colorful and very geometric, he was kind of a "Brito", when he wasn't even known, I thought Ron's paintings are more substantial and meaningful, -I attracted him with my artistic expressions I thought-it was easy to become friends and start dating, a walking distance from our neighborhood it was a promenade and a city place that was full of restaurants, shops and every weekend a live band used to play, so it was just easy for us to walk around and getting Italian food and then dessert while touristing our neighborhood. Saturdays were most favorite days, I wasn't watching movies on my own anymore, I got now Ron to share with me movies he never watched before, and I have seen it before so I could understand what was happening. The first thing he made me realized is how people who has lived all their lives in a peaceful country do not understand violence, it was an unknown ground for him to see war and death in a movie, He was asking me why I was crying over a movie …he said to me-that's not real-, but it is real, he didn't know therefore no room in his head to have those images, but I grew up in a place with war, violence and dead shootings. I did noticed his pure essence and I did like that from him, we were different, working in the same field sharing the same interest and totally different backgrounds, then I thought perhaps my painting are black because it was still some darkness in my thoughts … perhaps there are none, but it was good to see him and observe there was not trace of any evidence of violence in his surroundings, I felt jealous on some sort. I wanted to have those memories where violence didn't exist or at least only in movies.

It was Sunday, and we used to go to church together, then I didn't know why my emotions were so all over me while with him, I cried at church just by watching a mom caring for her son, perhaps I was projecting myself, and then I was happy after the service as I walked out and see the shiny sun, I think he was shock to noticed my moods and changes at the speed of a flash, and that is me. I didn't know I was an empath till much later-in life but I managed now to control my emotions by avoiding things that trigger them. An empath can feel and live any others people emotions just by observing, and it can be either happiness or sadness, good vibes or evil vibes…I specially avoid at all circumstances evil people, I just walk away from it right away, the sensation are heavy and shady and drains your energy easily. I think I was a kind of a rare animal to Ron, but it was fun and easy to be around, we helped each other out when needed, we were friends and now things starting to go to the next level.

It was Christmas and I was there in red at Ron's office Christmas party. I didn't know nobody and it was my first "office Christmas party" he was introducing me with his co-workers but it wasn't much to talk with my broken English and heavy latin accent, so greetings were short and conversations were either cut off or avoided by me. I remembered I was looking all around the place to see if I knew someone else besides Ron, and yes I saw a guy I knew. He was there and I felt like yay I am not a rare animal here. The guy approached me as he was observing me with intensity and purpose. He saw I was with Ron and he knew him as well, so it was easy for him to break and jump into me. I think that guy said the most stupid thing Ive ever heard but i didn't know the importance of that men in my coming future.

I was tired, the Christmas party seemed not to end, and food as usual in those weren't that good, not much people I know and therefore wanted to go home. Ron didn't want to go so I was off. I think I got home in less than 20 minutes, and the phone rang just as I laid in my bed. Ron seemed to not believe I was heading home, but then I was and he just said he just wanted to say goodnight and thanks for going to the party, I said i was thankful to got to go there and had my first experience of my new life and celebrating Christmas in the American way.

I think Ron traveled to his family for New Year's Eve, cause I don't really recall any major event that happened with him until it was February already, oh well when he came back I filled his unit door with welcome stickers in all languages, I felt doing something good for him and I really missed him, he came and he had a bad stomach-ace after having a mac; I have never had such a thing, but I eat the fries.

Valentines Day was approaching but I had this sensation Ron wasn't the man for me, I didn't want to spend that special day with someone I don't really think can be "really" be with me. Anyway I let it go and working days were filling in and so my English lessons, one day of any of those weeks Ron invited me for a walk and an ice cream, gelatos were close by and I do like those, so we went. We had the most awkward conversation as he was listening to my thoughts, I was mute and revolving my head with every word he was saying. He wasn't breaking up with me or anything similar but instead bringing me messages of the only person I knew besides him at the Christmas party. I think he was proud that his girlfriend was noticed by someone else and that guy really let him know he noticed me, that was an unknown arena for me, but life works in amazing ways, and the story of this book end just starts here.

"El circulo de la vida"

CHAPTER 9

My First Valentines Day

It was already February 2003, everything around me turned red and pink, hearts everywhere and even the drinks turned different colors and flavors. I had to admit America has its own way to celebrate and its wonderful, I don't think any other place in the world where celebrations are taking so seriously, even if some people call them other reasons, Ive always big on celebrations and Love is a beautiful thing to celebrate…then because of this thought a reasoning came to my head.

As big as Valentines might be for some, my focus are on them, and it is big for me, why to share it with someone isn't meaningful to you? I started myself asking that question, and then decided it wasn't worth it for me to keep up with a date that wasn't going to the same direction as I was, now what was that direction?…Started to wondering, so I guess is the time for me to be honest and tell myself what I wanted at the time.

I was feeling I wanted to have someone with me to share life and family. To me it has been always easy to get on track with my professional life and the kind of work that I do just flow, and finding that significant other with similar dreams and wants is a great deal, I wanted that great deal, who doesn't?

After the dissolution of my young marriage passed about good 3-4 years and I enjoy family life and family time while it last, so I guess I was looking for some kind of new partner to go and start a new family, that was my intention with the first marriage anyway and I thought this time with the experience I have it sure will be easier to find Mr. right one. I made a list of things wanted of course and I remembered trying to be very specific, and in all honesty for a 28 years old that list and knowing exactly what I wanted it was pretty good and crucial, so my American Dream wasn't getting a home or a great job and all the materialistic list of things I can achieve and I acquired them anyway myself...my American dream was and always have been to find someone to love and hopefully get loved back. I can say now while translating this book with certainty the search of everyone...each one of us is looking for that perfect or even imperfect match who will love hopefully unselfishly for whom you really are and with the intention of just growth older together and be each other company until it last. This happened to me in the first try and I was there for the second... hopefully this one will last longer-I thought-when making that decision of having someone and of course I also thought the worse thing could happen is that it could end, and of course I was there and continue living so lets try for that not to happen but nothing is under our control when feelings and emotions come.

Breaking up with Ron, wasn't an easy task specially close to San Valentin and on top of it his car broke. Ron dresses properly and crispy at all times, by the time I got into the car crash scene I saw a Ron I've never seen before, he was sweaty, kind of lost and no himself at all. We took care of the car accident and in my car off we went. His car will be at the car shop by a towing company next day first thing in the morning, I felt good I could help him, but I wasn't so happy as in my head I was just planing the break up moment. From now we ride together to our jobs, and in the afternoons we come back. Those days were a way destiny play with me, we got to get to know each other more, it was kind of a life situation and it happened with ease for us, but wasn't easy for me. Finally when the car was back I was able to tell him that I didn't want to see him anymore, as I got to know this new guy he introduces me to and we both shared the same plans of a life together I said i wanted to give it a try. I think he understood and agreed and off he let me go.

It was already that 2 weeks period; Roy and I had agreed to meet at certain point when we both were certain we wanted to be with each other, Roy invited me to dinner one time, after I called him from a business card he handled to me while I was working, The board of architects committee its not a fun place for a lot of architects in town but it was for me and Felipe -my partner- We were always laughing at this nonsense committee which looks more like the College Testing Bureau, those architects check on your design to make sure your design complies with certain standards, at the time the standard were that everything has to look Mediterranean, and so our restaurant extension with pergola in the rear and our climbing plant proposed was just perfect. When it was our time to present our project Roy asked his friends to let him check my work, he managed the situation and he was our judge. A judge that focus on the construction part of it rather than the design, this guy asked me to submit construction details and more worry about construction than design. And that was Roy. Back at the time it was November and close to Thanksgiving. At a second review I got the approval needed after a whole presentation with renderings, a borrowed laptop and ready to rock this guy. After my presentation was done and the committee approved he handled me his business card with his house number in the back. Next time I saw him was at Ron's Christmas Party.

While Ron was await in his new years get away with family I called Roy, perhaps I was curious and I wanted to know what this guys which was so persistent wanted with me, perhaps and most certainly I wasn't happy enough with Ron as he certainly had other priorities in his life.

So the dinner day came with Roy, and so our conversation. I have to say that I express myself with ease as I know what I want, how I want it and with whom I want it, I was so direct with Roy, like never in my life before, I had the time to express what I wanted and how I wanted, and he was a possibility...the only sentence he said was "nobody has talked to me this way ever in my whole life but I do like it and lets do it" so that was the manifestation of all my wants, my list and the partner of life I was looking for. After his reply I said that we need a couple of weeks off of each other in order to clean and resolve any pending situations with others...I was thinking of Ron, so I proposed my master plan and he agrees.

The meeting place was just my morning walking path, a close park with a little lake and a tiny bridge that witness my morning routine, finally I was walking towards my future a future I visualized a future with so many adventures and a sensation that this would be it for me.

While walking all those images of Ron starting to fade and disappear, I was thankful of his friendship and company, and I consider him a friend, a good friend but not more and so I quietly said goodbye. Since that day Roy and myself walked and lived together till the end. And so Valentine's Day was our first date as a committed for a future couple.

CHAPTER 10

Giving LOVE

Roy was coming from an abusive marriage, I can't say who was the abusive one, but certainly toxic. His confidence was very low, he was anxious and living in fear. His fears were at the time reduced at the fact he could it loss his job any time…something Roy has been always great at it.

His knowledge and savvy were inspiration to me to do better with my career and job, he knew where the error was just by looking at a set of plans. Most people don't even understand a blueprint, even some professionals draw a line without knowing is a trace of a real substance, and so consequences come and responsibility just fade.

I cared for Roy, I didn't have his eye for projects in plans but I knew he was broken somehow and I just wanted to love him, he did the same, we were in love for a great amount of time, we set our routine by living in my place on weekdays and in his over the weekends.

As we set into our routine and lives little doses of the truth starting coming out, first was his divorce, still in process, he explained to me in words he wanted to cover up and make it complicated but in all honesty is easier to talk with the truth and say someone is being a bitch or the other is being a dick, that will simplify arguments and situation will go straight forward to the point. From one side applause his diplomacy, in the other hand he wasn't that honest to me and that bothers me. I gave him sometime and trust him as a woman in love I was, but always my brains shows and I can only be stupid for a while. While caring and loving was our daily routine and all just came right for us, that divorce situation really got into me, and after being just in love and enjoying our lives I asked him to go and take care of the situation if he really wanted to be with me, I moved with my friend back as my place lease was done and I was already living in his place. We have decided to finish each one of our leases before moving to a place on our own, so was the plan and we were doing it.

The days at my friend house were not that good, I missed him terrible but I knew I was doing the right thing, my friend and her devil sister explained to me and open my eyes as to why a divorce can take so long, its always money they said…they also said it could be that the man was playing with me, or they still have business together and what have you… let me tell you something and a free advise…please don't let anybody to let you down and continue your journey as you fucking wish! Have to admit that the influence sometimes your friends project on you can be either harmless or painful fortunately for me I always know where do I stand and so it was. Apparently Roy's previous wife was holding her signature for the sake of some moneys in the bank, Roy didn't say that to me but I got to know the truth trough the years.

After I moved to my friend we continue seeing each other but not as much, I have plenty of time to focus on my business and studies again and able to continue setting my company and my affairs with the business, but he was filling my thoughts and I knew he has things to do and so I was expecting him and decided to giving some time to resolve and take care of the things he needed to care at the moment, the days were so slow for me, it was the end of the summer and i wasn't happy living again with my roommate, I started wondering and lots of "what if" came to my mind, which I stopped them and decide just hope for the best, I knew I love him already and I knew somehow we will be together, that was my hope that was my wish and as always shushes come true. All it happened in less than 2 months and so we were ready to be together again, he managed to resolve the divorce documents and he came to me with that divorce sentence as a trophy and with so much happiness and hope, and I was so happy and thrilled that my friends weren't right with their conspiracy theories.

CHAPTER 11

The marriage proposal

Octctober was the month of a lot of happenings, after that rocky summer of 2003 going back and forth with past and papers and divorce documents…we finally set together into a place close to our jobs and fun to be. Downtown Miami was a place to set for a while, with ocean views and walking distance places to eat and relax Roy and I started a beautiful journey together. Another thanksgiving was coming and then Christmas, he gave me the most wonderful gift someone can give you when you are a distant mother. He brought my child and on vacations we went. My first born child was 6 that year and I couldn't be happier to have him come and spend time with us, we, now three had so much fun and memories built were priceless to me.

My son used to come every 6 months to visit and spend a month or two with us, as his studies allow him and so his father. It was always hard for me say good bye again to my little kid, but somehow you start getting use to things and life continues in mysterious ways while finally all fall into place. It was time for my kid to go back and I was specially sensitive that time, January was short, but I then realized that now I have Roy in a more formal way, and we also have a place together and perhaps one day my son will come and stay with us, that was back then just a thought and a wish.

At the Miami International Airport, we were all happy and having a good time, and I specially observed Roy he was mindful of me and my feelings with the kid, I was falling every single day more and more for him and happy to be now with a caring and loving man that was there just for me. A blessing I thought.

By the time JC left it was almost time for Valentines Day again, again red and pinks hearts starting to appear again and I started to noticed them more as I go on my days…Roy and I favorite time was after we finish our working days, 6:00 pm was the most wanted time of the day and dinners, chilling times and home movies were our daily most precious routine, I wasn't expecting much for Valentines just a dining out perhaps but then it was 6:00 pm and the bell of this home of us rings. kind of strange as Roy has a key but i was happy he was there. He was there in a long interior corridor of a fancy building we used to live kneeled before me; I think I was mute and full of joy, I couldn't articulate a word but I know my expression was just of happiness and joy, those times I remembered now were very beautiful indeed and always grateful of all of these experience I lived with him.

This is exactly what I would like to extend as to keep with you, the happy moments you experiment and live are to be the one you could reply in your memories, instead of other moments that weren't no that significant. As I am translating this book right now, all those memories replied to me and more and more are coming as my fingers dance with this keyboard, the way we met, things we shared, things we lived together, the way we laugh and entertain, our trips, our family life, our plans and achievements, those moments will remain, and the memories are treasures to keep, no-one can take that away from me and as I go I'm grateful of all of those situations and experiences that made me happy and shape my memories with ease and joy.

CHAPTER 12

Kids

I've always had chosen among all my memories and experiences keep and store only the beautiful ones, and they are a lot. Other experiences that perhaps hurt me in some way I allowed time to heal and let them go from my soul in order for my heart to be free.

The most important thing to me is to live life to the fullest, with intensity and purpose, Integrity and to live every moment as if it is the last moment I do have, that is my philosophy, my motto a policy I decided one day to adhere to my way of living, being present and living this moment is a beautiful gift anyone can enjoy.

When I met Roy in that restaurant where all conversation for a future together happened, our kids came as a subject, of course a very important subject for us as we both had kids on our own. My idea of a life together with someone at the moment-I talked to Roy-was simply to enjoy life with my partner, I didn't have any intention of having any more kids, I already had one and in my list I specifically ask that that person will have a kid on his own as well so kids could be something done for us. As I expressed myself that was the only thing Roy objected and strongly felt that was important to him, and he did want more than one kid, which I listened and digest in the timeframe of a flash, I said okay, let's do that, he really wanted a boy as he already had a girl, and I thought I have a boy and I would love to experience having a girl, so the math was easy and I agreed to have 2 one boy and one girl. and thats the pitch story of how Roy & Sophie came into our lives.

Our kids were apart from us as a result of our previous divorce, we only can enjoy them every other time, and we both appreciated and enjoy family time, so having kids on our own was excited and high hopes started to fill our days. Nati and JC visited us and we did enjoy as much as we could, but it always felt they were somehow borrowed as they didn't live with us.

Things will accommodate as life continues, I always thought, so I wasn't worried as I envision ed at some point my kid will reunite with me again, and he did.

18 months after I married my second son was born. Ive experimented an amazing real first moment with this kid, it took me to understand how babies are full and capable of understanding and awareness even when they in the womb.

3 days or so past after I was able to be home again, the hospital was a place to deliver the baby roomy and overall adequate but nonetheless a cold place with strangers helping you with something so intimate and important, I remembered kindness and nice words from nurses and doctors, spacious suite and a quite peaceful ambiance I could appreciate, but nothing compares to be home. So the moment came to feed my baby for the first time at home, I was preparing myself with a nice warm bath, the bathrobe was cozy and new, baby Jr was ready to sleep that portion of the night after his night bath and expecting to be fed before going to sleep. I took him from the crib next to my bed and sat at my bedside. My son looked at me as he has never seen me before. He was looking straight to my eyes wondering where he was and who I was, I just saw that in his beautiful new eyes, as I exposed and offered my nipple to him he was just starring at me with those questions, I couldn't help but to offered him the answers right away. I walked him throughout the house and as I carry him was explaining the spaces and some important items in the house, as pictures of his siblings and walking space by space to give him the sense that we were in our own place and now it was his as well. He was looking at me avidly and at the same time looking all his surroundings, he was paying attention to me, then when I sat again at the bedside and I had to explain I was his mom but now with clean and fresh smell clothes, at the hospital it was a blue standard robe and sweaty body, and now he just

couldn't recognize me. My son was pleased with answers and explanations I gave and so he accepted to be fed.

The pureness of his heart, the power of his awareness and understanding of who he is make this kid so special to me. And as my second kid I started to understand the differences and to respect that human being are so unique. Till these days Jr. continues to amazed me with his answers and actions, nothing like a parent won't feel for they kid but respectful of others I really think my son exceed average standards.

So then SAM came up, after 2 years or so and one miscarriage SAM took literally everything out of me, she took my essence I felt one day after a really intense morning sickness. I got that sensation that she was feeding herself with all I had, and cravings started all over the place and in all kind of types. Sam is a sweet smarty pants girl on her own, an updated version of myself perhaps, most people say that. I didn't know girls take that much from the biological part of us but with my girl that totally happened. Her ways and her actions are of a very creative soul, her ease with good things and what's right for her is just a symphony that I listen and is playing at all times, she bring me messages that I need to hear.

Amazed me how kids of the same parents can be so different, we humans are a very rare species, and a beautiful and unique one. Im grateful for my kids; from Roy and that second marriage I got this wonderful gift and I can't be more grateful for it.

My eldest son and first child, at the time of this book translation is dead, I guess I need it to write as perhaps there is still something in me that it needs to go out, Its being 2 years and little bit than a month and I didn't cry much, I accepted his departure and respect his decision, I found it he was a very decisive kid, I never understood why he didn't valued his life, he gave himself to others so much but for him was very little, his friends sent me all kind of messages and prepare a beautiful video that make me feel proud of him, and to me that was enough, knowing that my kid left a valuable lesson to others and he is remembered with full heart by his fellow friends make me feel good. As a mother I missed him, and I also feel I did my all to him, I was genuine and supportive when he needed, straight and clear when I needed to be. I chose to be happy and not getting depressed, life continues and so I came to realized that I only had two choices, be happy and continue with my life or depressed and get sick and be a pain to me and to others, I choose to be happy and accept what happened with respect and love.

Wherever you are my son, my heart and thoughts of the most beautiful moments are with you, perhaps you will read this book in a different time, and you will understand that you were very much loved and learn that life is the most precious thing we have to value and that we can't take it for granted, we are so used to live our lives without noticing that every day is a gift, a gift to give, a miracle that happen every morning when we open our eyes, we are here to light our lives and perhaps if lucky enough shine the life of others. So wherever you are, be the light and shine, you always liked colorful lights and the sparkles they project; and now you are a sparkle to me, a bubble that absorbs the sun light, a candle that I observe to burn and a bulb that is just lighting up. And I am letting you go, I've thought I did but now it seems official. Always love mom.

CHAPTER 13

The Middle East

Now from 2022 let's get back again to where I left. It was 2008. The real estate market in the US crashed. I think I put all of you back again. Stories of the properties being foreclosed, Chinese drywall and short sales were all over the place, but not for me, not for us not for my family. The market Crashed and a great opportunity was presented to us.

I was a Dillards with Roy shopping for a contemporary suit for him as he was called for an interview in New York, his company was about to offer him an overseas job, that man that I saw once with little confidence and fear of losing his job, was now a confident man and proud he got an opportunity like this, I was so happy and encourage him to expend in a nice looking gray suit, and of course I already have expressed to him that was all the way for it, kids were little, perfect time to travel and be overseas and besides over here people and friends were only talking BS about the economic situation and after his interview we were just adding moneys to the adventure to come, we started getting ready for a rich adventure in the Middle East.

As I always said and so Esther Hicks and all this law of attraction teachers, all happens for our greatest good, and I just saw it that way, things aren't working here lets go there where things are working better, and so a great door open for us, we were a young family supporting each other and working as a team, what else could we wish for? We were in tuned and all things played well for us. Always remembered that is just how you take and digest things that comes to you; by knowing that universe cares for all of us and all the way, nothing will happen to us that isn't intended for the greatest of, so with that thought I went and so my family.

Now the idea of the Middle East was to land in Dubai, glamorous Dubai with its own Palm Tree Island and a replica of this Bahamas hotel called The Atlantis, yes there is one exactly the same over there, and The Burj Al Arab, tallest building now, all of that was so excited and new for us and of we went.

To our surprise we got business tickets to Jeddah, Kingdom of Saudi Arabia, I didn't even know that existed, but Roy did, he used to work with a petroleum company in his younger years in Tampa, and he was designing petroleum plants and what have you for some well known Arabic companies and Texas related groups, he explained to me it was a wealthy country, so I just saw it was very closed to Dubai, and it was enough reference point for me.

Roy had to go first get settled and prepare things for my arrival and the kids, The Middle East is a very different animal, is a kind of Latin culture but with more moneys and very reserved education, till the nineties people were riding camels, and so basically infrastructure was a thing of the latest nineties and early millennium, we are architects so basically for us was Legoland. So now the idea of Jeddah, we didn't know but all I heard was that it was the most cosmopolitan city of KSA, surrounded by the Red Sea and very close to North Africa, locals past their chilling times in Sharm AL Sheik and some northern cities close to the Mediterranean coast. For us was just a very different playground.

Once Roy settled and was ready to get us in, I started my journey with he kids, my trip wasn't ideal as I had to do couple of stops before landing in Jeddah, I was so excited getting to know new places and different cultures, so the whole planning trip and the trip itself was exciting and thrilling...till I landed in Egypt as my last stop before getting to my new place of living.

Perhaps it was already midnight I guess and while changing planes we were sweaty, the business class trip from New York to Madrid and then from Madrid to Egypt was just pleasant and smooth, but all that seem to fade as we were running through a tiny corridor to board our plane, business class didn't have any lounges nor limousines to drive you to the gate, it was just so other countries, everything started to become so real and I just couldn't wait to just get to my new home. The trip to Jeddah was short, and or perhaps I fall asleep and so my little ones. Landing at the airport and getting into immigration things started to get even more real, women disappear from my eyesight, I only saw burkas and covered heads with black abayas, it was striking to me, men seem to control everything and the few woman were passengers that from the plane to landing just change their attires in the most blocking way. Ive never experience anything like that I couldn't see any woman eyes at all, so I felt so naked just wearing this abaya my husband had sent it previously but couldn't imagine wearing that thing and covering my whole face including the eyes. So I say to myself Welcome to the Middle East.

The-jet-lagged last 2 or 3 days, the excitement to get to know the place got into me and I wanted to be out and about. First the compound we got to live in was where the most American used to live, so it was safe, okay and apparently a hot spot to be by the local society standards of the city, it was okay we were together and that made me happy. Expats from all over started to gather at the park and for happy hour time I will say at the local restaurant and tennis court, oh there was a bowling alley as well, we had everything there. Spaniards, Italians, Asians, Americans and of course the Lebanese. We were from all over the places, to me that was lots of fun, new country, new culture, tons of people, the possibilities seems endless for us to be there for a while.

Routine started and so I found myself in a breakfast morning reunion full of women only…not men, they were working and we gather at those breakfast to talk shoes and bags I didn't know that was it for a girl like me…so when they asked me what did I do and introduced myself I said I am an architect and I am looking for a job. One of the ladies jumped and said she knew someone who was looking for help in her office, the sound of that were music to my ears, so I said woman worked here too, I'm glad, cause I will love to work here and have a different experience, I am a mother a wife but also a career woman, so Rachel helped me with that endeavor of mine that just popped up at the time of finding myself there while doing very little, eating a lot and talking shoes.

Tactile Design Studio was a little Interior Design Studio owned by couple of friends, and it came handy that an American woman appeared to help at a most wanted moment as the company was growing and none of those woman seemed to have time to handle the business properly, Senior designer Hania was practically managing great part of the business but some of the things were just out of her hands and simply put it-she wasn't available to deal with-I was glad I could catch immediately what was needed from me, and then my journey started and I was so happy and glad I found a niche I could express myself professionally and able to help with an endeavor I was for sure capable of.

Hania was managing the residential part of the business and I was there to handle all commercial projects and help with the office management, -piece of cake-I thought and so I did, for over 2 years I was handling this company and overseeing the commercial part of it which was in the health services industry hospitals and health centers to be more specific, all of them in the Middle East. It was a great journey, full of places to visit, projects to tackle and hospitals to open and old places to renovate and update. The company was booming and its new client and I was a very important piece in the making of this happening and therefore a lot of wealth in the form of moneys came to me and my family. It was fun for sure and very productive times. My head is transporting me there with all the business trips, meetings with board members and hospital directors and mostly men and myself without burka and colorful abayas despite the locals with the boring blacks and unnoticed colors, I think I myself spice up Jeddah with a new trend in colorful abayas, a fashion that my girlfriends in the compound applaud and celebrate with me while refreshing ourselves with mint frozen lemonades at the open terrace of the Arabian Homes Restaurant.

2 years went fast, summer was the time to get out of Jeddah and come back where home was, after 2 years of living in a different country a mentality start to shift and for me those 2 years marked something that was about to end.

I now knew how was to live there, work there, gather with friends and expats and traveling as a form of scape, I knew the wealthiest families, we were mingled with the high society and my husband was working with the Bin Laden family, what a journey.

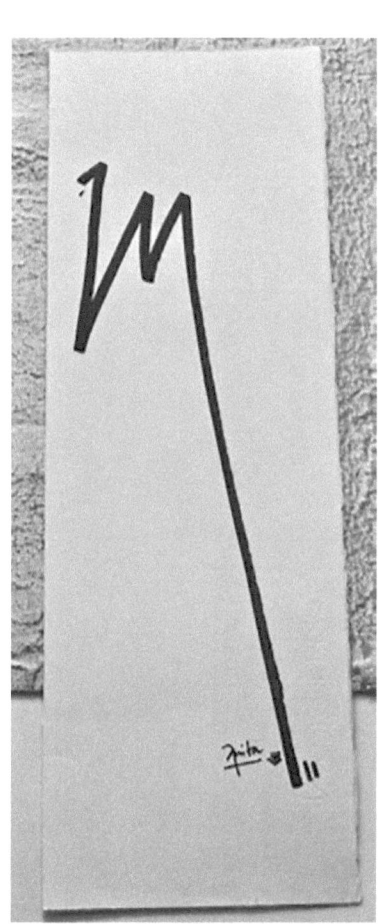

"Camellos", marcador en papel de acuarela.

CHAPTER 14

My Travels

L ove traveling, and thank you to my experience of living in the Middle East for over three years my world just expanded. Throughout my years I have counted I've been in over 40 countries, and 5 continents, however there almost 200 countries in the world and 2 more continents to explore and I am not even close to the 25% portion of the number, I used to said I have 160 more to go but now, I just want to be home, there is this song that I love to listen called Ya Rayah by Rachid Taha, I couldn't help but to listen to that song over and over again after my years of living in Jeddah, the song refers to a traveler that is looking for new adventures and avoiding fate or destiny in their own place, or some sort to my understanding. I came to realize with that song that perhaps other breeze will blow for me now. A new adventure a new thing to do and enjoy as much.

Europe is exciting and beautiful and so many places with so much rich culture to know, but I also get the sensation that I never get enough and when planning to go again I just don't seem to find the time. Spain, France, Italy the Blue Coast, the Mediterranean Sea and countries along, all those beautiful places I have visited got into my memories and love the thought that nobody will take that from me, one day while driving and observing at Sorrento rocky mountains border in Italy I just realized that all places seems to look alike. From Colombia, South America and the Andes Mountain range to the Arabian Sea and passing by the Alpes to learn how to ski were so much to enjoy, getting to know old pyramids in Gitza Egypt, and in Mexico, I said I love the Chichén Itzá from Yucatan as it has more architecture and craftsmanship to show but then again Gitza seems to hide secrets and numbers as clues of the history of the world, its just amazing how all places have their history and that we get to know and enjoy seems just priceless and wonderful as the sphinx without nose doesn't seem to appealing to me neither those piles of stones crafted with precision, I was there and memories reply as time have never passed. Thats the beauty fo our brain, and images we catch, encourage all what you see, explore and be grateful to your vision, to your brain, to the senses that are there for you 24/7 and allow you to enjoy, smell and touch all there is around.

What I have learned for my travels? To travel first class or at least business, to get a small suitcase-every place I go they sell clothes and shoes-everywhere so a lighter bag will do best, explore new food and flavors, be open and wild with your taste, at the end rice and beans are cooked everywhere. There is a time for everything and nothing, there are days you want to be out and about, there are quite days you want to be enjoying you balcony view and there are days you just want to be in bed watching old movies and soap-opera shows...do as you wish, relax yourself in the now, and when you wish for something just be certain it will come, so be careful or not of the places you want to be as they will bring you more experiences and richness to your life and at the end of some travels you just want to be home.

Now I've decided to become a pilot, so it will be easy for me to go places as I wish and to escape and relax close to nature and oceans I enjoy. So my taste in traveling the world changes as I go, therefore I go easy with myself with the choice Im making at the present moment and who knows perhaps I will reconsider again 160 more countries I would love to see, for now I focus my attention of my private pilot license, cause its giving joy and excitement as I am trying something totally new.

I have shared some of the pics in this book as they were meaningful to me in one way or another, perhaps they inspired you to go and explore new places or perhaps they will make you wonder how life will be in a different place. I hope you enjoy them and stop yourself for a moment or two to appreciate what is in front of you, and create a new reality to explore, whatever makes you happy just do, whatever takes you to dream and be present enjoy, Happiness is within you, is not the places you haven't been that will give you that, is all you and the decision to be who you really are, so go get naked and be clear of the things you really want and discern calmly what is that is keeping it from doing it, you will find all your truths within the reach of a thought and wanting to do it will be just enough to keep you moving and thrilled to the completion of your wanting. Be You, Do less Have more!

CHAPTER 15

My first born child

As the third year in Kingdom of Saudi Arabia-KSA-started to shape for me, certain thoughts appeared and I was aware of all of them. My first child who was living in the country we both were born was getting in his teen years and now more open to express his decisions of where he wanted to be. I was expecting since I left the country in 2002 for my son to be with me and now 9 years later appeared to be the time and the rhythm of events were guiding me to that wish of mine.

Sometimes in life you lose something to gain greatest things, never be afraid of loosing something, just be certain something grater is forming and will manifest soon for you. In the pursuing of having my eldest son living with me I tried everything, first I wasn't sure to establish myself in Saudi Arabia for so long, we as a family spoke to be there for some period of time, we never discuss the years but it was implied that wasn't meant to be for long.

After living in a different place for over 2 years you really start wondering if that place is the place you want to stay, and in all honesty to me KSA was just a stopping point something that appears to us but as the culture is very different and the weather is intense no expat wants to live there for longer, we go there for the money and the opportunities, is a good place to save money and travel around and learn other cultures but you missed home, and America has been home for me and still is.

So JC my son, was ready to live with us and so as excited as I was I couldn't help but express my happiness everywhere, my worldwide friends support me in the task of "you need to be where your heart is"…Roy wasn't in the same page, apparently he wanted me to stay and I didn't know for how much longer but definitely longer, money at my job was good so he merely see everything with a money sign and I just saw everything with my heart as a mom. I tried for my son to join us in KSA, but something drastic had to happened. In order for my son-who was conceived from a previous marriage-live with us and have a Saudi visa, he must be the legal son of my present husband, in other words he had to give up his biological father paternity. So go figure.

So another plan took place, and shared my thought with Roy and I think that was some sort of the beginning of an end. My plan was to come back to America bring the kids of course and bring my eldest kid as well from Colombia, Roy will stay for 2 more years as he also had expressed he dint wanted to stay for much longer and in the meantime I could help him to see which opportunities will arise for him while in US. To me it was a no brain decision, my son was involved, and so he was part of me, and I have this amazing opportunity now to be and share with my first born child and recuperate some time we lose together while in his younger years. When I came to this country I expressed in a previous chapter wasn't easy to live away from him but I accepted and with the hope that someday will happen and all things will fall into place I went, so that moment so much expected was here…and feel blessed and fortunate however Roy did not see it that way.

I arrange with my son he will land in US about the same time we will arrive after our summer vacations, a Mediterranean cruise I booked for me and my family and that was my farewell for all those years in KSA and my way to celebrate another chapter in the book of my life.

The house in America became small now with three kids all of them different ages and sexes. Jc arrived in the middle of the summer of 20011 full of joy and thrilled to start a new life with me and his siblings, we used to see JC every summer and winter for vacation time but now he will be with us 24/7 it was excited for all of us, school arrangements took place, setting the house and just us being a family started to happened. Meanwhile Roy was there with us but far away in his thoughts, I did see it but that was something it didn't bother me as I was more focus of making my son feel comfortable with us. A shadow of non conformity sense once by looking at Roy in his eyes, I couldn't do much the decision was made and plan was in course. We were now a family of 5 and soon Roy will let us to be away from us for at least 2 years.

I have never regret this decision I made, even if it costed me other things, to me other things weren't strong as I thought they were to overcome this piece of happiness I grabbed as part of being a mom, I am a mother and as such I honor that with the responsibilities it comes, and it was the time for me to stand for my son and I did.

JC lived a life full of changes with a dad that perhaps bad mouth me but at the end it is what it is, I was able to try and do the best I could for my son, and by worrying about what else I can do for him to make him feel more comfortable perhaps I didn't listen to some of his requests, when a time came and he was already in his first year of high school I changed his school as we moved to a bigger house, and blinded by the accessibility and convenience didn't listen to his request-when he said he wanted to stay where he was-I did the best I could at the time things happened, sometimes in the pursuing of trying to do more we actually do less and that was something I learned, life is full of lessons and I never stop learning, learning from my actions, from the actions of others close to me, and for the most part for the decisions we make and the way they impact our lives, however as a responsible party for all my decisions I stand for what I believe is true and good and never feel regrets because I know those decisions were crafted with the best intentions and love, but my son gave me a lesson to listen more.

He was able to finish high school and combine a part time job with his college studies, he did good and he was finding his ways, and I decided to let him be him, and now I just flow with my youngest kids and allow them to walk at their own pace; he is not with us anymore but I am glad all I did for him was with the best intention and love I have.

May his soul be light in another dimensions and peace remain with him always and forever.

CHAPTER 16

Public Service

Life is a recipe and the ingredients are those things that we like, we need and we want, a balanced amount of the ingredients allow a pretty good result.

Balancing life has been a very important topic to me, I certainly believed that fulfilling all the aspects in life that are important to us will lead to a happy, peaceful and meaningful way of living. Nonetheless work and family seems to take great chunk of the pie we must strive to achieve and fulfill other parts of us in order to find balance and a life lived with meaningfulness and purpose and that will give us so much joy and gratification.

Once settled in town with my kids and the new home I wanted to continue working even though Roy said lets focus on the kids and don't do much, I think I don't listen to things that I don't want to hear, pretty simple, I am my own person therefore able to make decisions on my own. I wanted to work in a way I managed my own time and be available for my kids if they need me, that's why I started to explore what I could do in order to fulfill my spare time, while looking for options I was called to participate in an education committee for the town I was living at, it was a great start as I always like to be a force for the community, a voice that can be heard to help others.

When Ann Gerwig-now Major of Wellington-asked me to volunteer at that education committee as liaison while she was planning and doing her running for mayor candidature I immediately say yes, in fact my son was victim of bullying at school and I was finding options and doors to open for finding solutions, it was just something I manifest while doing always what I feel passion about.

Among several issues we discussed at this committee, it came to my attention that very little were discussed about the drugs consumption and supply in high schools, sexual encounters and smoking, those were things I was worried about as this was so new to me, and so to my kid; but apparently these people just see those issues as part of the high school years. I came to realize that our culture allow so many things that in nature and principle aren't right, one thing is allowing and giving space to your kids but another thing is to conspire by let them decide in things that might need more communication and a different approach in order for them to make a sound choice. So, decisions, that to me, as the kids are under age, we parents can control were just let unattended, and it was heartbroken seem nobody seem to care at a point I was making.

Accepting you can't change things you can't control is a major undertaking, life has taught me that sometimes the best action is not action at all, and what we can't control we release to the universe so it will take care of, and we-humans-manage somehow to discern the information and lesson given in the form of listen to other chanels of communication. As much as I enjoy helping my community sometimes we need to step back and put all in the Universe vortex so life will take care of its own and in a more playful ways, which I have happened to learn to observe and appreciate as they manifest in front of me.

CHAPTER 17

Healthy Foods

Between couple of meetings per month with the education committee and taking care of my kids daily that was pretty much the activities filling my calendar, trying to find a way to make my kids eat more vegetables was the challenge of the moment, I still had plenty of time and wanted to do something on my own, I remembered I used to walk around the community we were living at and certain day by looking around I spotted an abandoned restaurant next to the club house and activity center. I have always have passion for food and cooking, so it was fun for me preparing meals daily and always thinking what was best for my kids to eat, we weren't into any fast food nor sodas or cheesy snacks, I was all about more natural and healthy habits but trying to approach them with a more fun way, spotting and abandoned restaurant was kind of a first sign for what the future will bring us next.

Back in 2012 healthy habits in foods just started as collective consciousness in the East Coast of Florida, not even close but for me was huge and I remembered the only healthy items available were smoothies and grass shots, Not so promising.

At home was basically cooking meals, and as I go, was thinking of ways to make food healthy but tasty and fun so my kids will eat it and get the nutrients they need, I also did it for myself I have to say, having lettuce and spinach everyday to keep myself healthy wasn't appealing and I finally developed a soup recipe my kids were so happy to eat and I hide in it all ingredients they didn't like and for some reason wont eat, then I did with lentil soup and then with tomatoes, so it was a win-win situation and I was so happy and thrilled I found the secret so my kids will eat vegetables and for myself the soups were a treat and a get away of the very single day salad; and all of that happened without the hazard and the fights around the dining table, we were a happy family eating well and having a great time.

I have learned from experiences and my readings that illness in the body comes as a result of emotions we don't express, I have been reading a great deal of books and authors, doctors and inspirational speakers about the subject and its just so appealing to me and resonate with the fact that indeed is not the food we eat that make us sick but the emotions and anger we don't express; that combined with poor eating habits it is just a bomb to our organism.

I've always wanted to make sure my kids express themselves, and they do, all the time and I was happy I was raising kids weren't afraid to talk or say anything and everything.

When I came from the Middle East I was overweight, and I remembered I used to blame my condition with Thyroids for that specific fact, but as I decide one day that that wont be an excuse anymore for me to be in great shape all started to change, started with yoga classes and mindfulness, and I came to realize that in the last year of my stay in the Middle East I wasn't talking to Roy much, I didn't express lost of things I had just because I didn't want to get into arguments with him, and so all went to my throat were words wont come out and I stopped them there, all kind of clergies to food also starting to appear, and I was bother by that I couldn't eat gluten, and the collective called "celiac Disease" dairy products, collective call "lactose intolerance" pineapple and honey...it went far and I just wanted to know why all suddenly changes in me starting to appear. Most of friends and family members-who don't know better-told me all kind of stories that I just didn't believe, so on a journey I went to find out what was wrong with me.

Louise Hay was the first one I listened too, and all her words resonated to me 100% I didn't pay attention to other conditions but paid close attention to those that applied to me, it totally make sense I thought. I wasn't expressing myself with words to Roy as I knew he wont listen and so I kept words, things I should said were unspoken and so all went to my throat and get stuck there. So the condition with my Thyroid became worse. As per the allergies I was denying my own power and just letting him control me somehow…and remembered I felt kind of guilty with the decision of coming back, humans have their way to manipulate and control, and it is up to us to allow them or stop them.

It was a concept hard for me to understand if someone really love you they will try to manipulate you, that's actually lack of love, but I didn't realized that at the time, I was so busy wanted to get cured, for sure things started to change and I could see deeply and clear that his old habits and situations weren't totally resolved and he was projecting on me. I was glad I spotted the situation and of a journey oh healing I went.

Yoga and meditation have served me well, most people are not fiends with gyms, and its okay, we just need to find what we like to do and do it, and that my fiends apply to everything, how we exercise, how we eat, how we connect with people, how we express ourselves…we all unique and so go easy with you and don't keep on trying things you wont like, they only will make you miserables and resistant to a situation you wont need. Be kind to yourself, love the self and ask what do you want to do today? Sometimes the answer can be, just rest and sleep, our bodies talk to us in so many ways and sometimes as we are so busy with the routine, we don't listen and care, and the body will at some point stop and rebel, be easy and flow with your senses and the way you feel, there is no better medicine.

I started to pay more attention to that abandoned restaurant while walking to my yoga class and now I just realized was the way I saw myself, abandoned and sad inside, with a nice facade and location, craving for some TLC.

CHAPTER 18

Anita's Cafe Bistro

On a family dinner while I share with my kids that the community had an abandoned restaurant they just jump in it and said lets open a restaurant mom!…it will be like a having a big kitchen and living room and we can feed everyone…my kids-lego lovers-started to make restaurants and kitchen with legos and share with me the way it had to look, I was so excited with the idea and I had the money to start and ready to roll in this new thing, however it was a conversation I needed to have with Roy before anything going further; and I was hesitant to share it with him, he has this way to say "no" to everything we ask him, his first answer is always no… so I did know what his answer will be so I decided to go a step further, I have to say it! and understanding myself and the healing process I was experimenting, I now was feeling more capable to speak out and express all my wants and needs and feelings at once.

The step further I took before having this conversation with Mr. No, was to find all information I can gather about this restaurant there. So I met Cliff and then the whole board members committee, bunch of manipulative people who at the time were very helpful and nice and to these days I still grateful for the opportunity they gave me to open a restaurant while I healed myself.

I ended up negotiating with them for a very ridiculed rent amount, nobody would say no, not even Mr. No. Expenses to update the restaurant to my standards they offered to pay, utilities and what have you was almost covered by them, it was just a no brain decision and I was all for it.

My kids were so happy, specially Sophie this little thing was not even 6 but she understood what we were doing and it was all fun for her, they were my helpers, they designed everything and shape it for me. I just follow instructions from my kids.

It was the time to have the conversation with Roy as the boards members will present me to the community but all of them said it will be okay if you want it you get it, so the community presentation was just a cordiality, something politically correct to do, and I did. As I was explaining to Roy and get his support I explained in detail all the scenarios and situation and the terms, and even him couldn't say no. We were all on board, a relief for me and so to a new adventure we went

The concept of the restaurant for me was clear and straight, we wanted to offer healthy choices with yummy flavors, kind of a mediterranean bistro with an American twist, it was clear to me, not to the board committee who were supporting my business, -at least that was I thought-so then a series of truths starting to come out to the surface and I ended up knowing that they wanted me to sell bagels for breakfast, sandwich for lunch and pizza for dinner.

They didn't know with whom they were dealing with and my latino blood half Indian, half white and with a spaniard trace came to place. I stand for my beliefs and trues even if they mean to go against some, I can care less but I wont let anyone to tell me what to do, this was a clean business transaction for me, but their intentions were otherwise.

As I refused to do at theirs wishes, I learned they will stop supporting me, i had a contract for 2 years and basically they have control, but my business didn't go down, and they had to respect the terms, the whole community loved the idea, the place, the restaurant concept and of course the food, only few were not on board, I started to know these people, once I thought they were more sophisticated than that, knowing the truth and have the clarity of what people want is a sixth sense I have developed throughout the years and heck it serves well. When you are in tuned with your higher self it is very easy to understand the dark secrets the others kept, they just appear and revealed to you so easy and flawless that a plan of attack it is easy to explore and manifest.

Anita's Bistro were not out of business because of this group of people, after a little more than a year when my husband returned he came with an offer to work back in Miami, and again was a family decision to be altogether as a family supporting each other-or him- and live happily ever after. As another new chapter started I was selling the business with all happy customers and my loyal accountant wondering what that kind of decision was coming that from. Again I chose to do what I wanted to do, and what I thought it was right to do, no matter what happens I choose my family again, knowing that the decision was already a win. I healed myself from my allergies while working hard in the restaurant, it was great that amount of work I did with passion and joy and on top brought me to a perfect fit, totally worth it, after a while I felt I won again, and off the restaurant business I was.

Another experience I lived, a beautiful and yummy one, my kids remember that with joy and hope we will open the One next.

CHAPTER 19

Together again

As my husband reunited again with the family after 2 years overseas, all of us were happy to be together again, I was still putting myself together after giving up on the restaurant. I was only hoping my broken love still have the impulses to go all the way all over again. A broken love as I saw a man sick and locked to himself and everyone else, a broken love that was trying to continue, a broken love that I understood I was the only one giving.

When people are away from themselves a lots of issues surface, anger, resentment and unwilling to forgive and love again appear. A series of "now I know" theories play all the important roles, and I know all of them are expressions of the ego.

Our marriage started to fill heavy and uneasy, only looking for places to go and booking vacations to escape from ourselves, but they we were, together again vacationing, at first can be fun going to places and enjoy with the kids, after a while if your significant other isn't in the same page is not the same, kids were part of me, a part of me, not all of me, my husband was another part of me, but again not the whole me, career, kids and playing time was covered but a part of me that is important as all of the others wasn't fulfilled.

One booking after the another and another and places here and there till one day said no more.

Our last trip to Alaska as a family was nice to me, I explored a new place, I enjoy the iced picks and the wild flowers, our last cruise ship to Alaska in summer 2017 brought me memories of the Mediterranean one in 2011, but this one was specially cold, and it wasn't only for the weather back there, but our hearts were so distant and separate from each other. It wasn't fun, I was not happy, I didn't enjoy the way I always do, and all of that just felt wrong.

The 4th of July at the Miami International Airport was fun, I was happy I got back home, at least it was room to breath in the hotel and cruise ship wasn't that much space. My first words to Roy at the moment we landed and we pick up our luggage were "please do not book more vacations with me, you can do it with the kids but please do not include me" that was clear to me that I just didn't want to experience any of those moments I had, we were not a couple anymore, we were trying to hold together for the kids, but the glue wasn't that good anyway.

Kids are amazing and they were happy but mom have told them prior to the trip that perhaps mom and dad will split...I have always had spoke the truth to my kids and to anyone, even if it hurts, even if its not the right time, to me to telling the truth and speaking as it is do not come with a list of instructions, you just say it, and it feels so good, so easy and therapeutic.

Of course I was worried about my kids, but I was more worry about myself, if I am not well what good can I do to others?

That is my intake about my wellbeing and the wellbeing of others, first me, then the rest, even if it sounds selfish, we ought to please ourselves first in order to do good for others, its so clear, the sign at the airplanes clearly reads "first put your masks before helping others" and that apply to everything.

So I put my mask so I could breath well and into another journey I went.

It wasn't as easy as it is written here, ending a relationship, a family with kids and a routine is a challenging thing to do, however I would like all of you to know that every change that comes into your life is always for the better, and you grow out of it and more wonderful things unfold for you, when time passes you will appreciated more and understand better, but you have to know now to learn to accept it with the best of you.

Knowing that everything happens for your highest good nothing else will bother in your life again.

Roy had a lot of issues to solve on his own, and as he said one day to me, if a human is surrounded by shit, shit is all they have to spread. I just couldn't handle his shit no more. I am also have to say that I am very grateful and appreciative of all the times, adventures and kids we had together, he is a good man, perhaps just not good enough for me. My standards now are much higher and that's all thanks to him.

CHAPTER 20

Plan A

I am plan A. me me me, healing myself, finding myself again, and polishing my edges better. It will be at the end Anita 2.0. I will continue choosing the experiences I would like to live, choices without labels I will make, and those will be beautiful experiences to me, since a little girl always wanted to explore and continue to do so, my heart hasn't changed and nothing that has happened to me, -now I know-wont change it a bit, its my secret, give my all always and forever, without reservations and marks from the past, every day is a new one to start just will learn to vibrate in higher frequencies when only stars will shine.

I hugged myself, I'm holding on to continue with this journey of my life, every knowledge, every experience that made me laugh, learn and live had taken me here, and all of those at the same time keep me going to do more. I feel myself with love and gratitude with the fountain of love is within me, it doesn't matter that I love and they don't love me back, I know where to fill myself and love is all I have to spread. With love and gratitude continue to reach that dream, that dream of mine that since little I continue to wait for. With love as my shield that's nothing to fear, I live, I love, I play, I win, I go, I do and just yesterday realized this formula will laid here, Be You, Do less, Have more.

It is with a great joy, now that I've decided to start a new life on my own and my main goal is me...I just can see only good things coming my way.

I want to learn to dance with nature, with trees with waters and winds and perhaps if lucky enough I can became one of them.

CHAPTER 21

Live again, always do

What is out there for me? Only good things I know, so many things, but what I really need is here within me, I don't need nothing more. I am enough.

The air is here and it helps me breathe, the tiredness make me rest, the hunger make me eat, the sky covers me and the sun shine my days, the waters refreshes me and the earth connects me to give all that I have to give and say all what I have to say.

Without expectations and presumptions, without egos and vanity I will stay here, it is my happy place, I am here with the now telling me just to finish these ending lines.

Places to go will how up, more food to eat and recipes to create will try…perhaps-who knows-wherever I go and the wind blows I now know the way it goes. Another languages to speak another people to know and from time to time a piece of something I would take in order to remember it was.

My art I will continue to craft, with this heart of mine in pieces for now, will learn to mend, it is what it is, and so new things will come to live, to learn to create to evolve and one day a healing soup will make spread for those that need to heal.

Logo "The Healing Soup", Anita / Amazing seven studios

CHAPTER 22

The Power of Love

For the power of Love this Book was born. For Love my passion burns, because of love I learned to forgive and because of Love I found the Truth.

This living and now written True moves me and will move You. You have come this far to find and apply as well.

Laws and guidelines by humans are done, and also a human will undo, You, Us can create and destroy its just a choice for what you want to be, a light to shine? or a fire that destroy?, is all up to you, and I would like you to understand that murder aren't only those that shot a gun, there are people that kill hopes, pure hearts and they just walk around like meek animals.

Another Dream, and I just woke up.

Today is another day and I am in love again, in love with life, night and day here or there, everywhere anywhere I am and I will be.

While seating here and surrounded by blues of the skies and the oceans that surrounds me, observe these humans passing by, walking, running, talking and yielding, busy and observing and my only wish is that we all learn to Love.

CHAPTER 23

The grief

Its being 9 months since I took the painful decision but smart choice of getting divorce. Remember one thing is always 2 things, just find the other end, and accept that all is well.

Today I came to realized that the pain this love has caused me is that I gave it and I never asked for the delivery receipt. Perhaps by acknowledgment of receipt I will have a proof that I give it, and perhaps is too late. I don't know that was just a thought, and as such I am letting it go.

I read this morning right after my healthy breakfast in this beautiful place I am enjoying and is helping me heal, that "Being deeply loved by someone gives you strength, while loving someone deeply gives you courage" Lao Tzu.

I understood by default that courage was all it was, but I also understood-and this is most important-that I've been loved by the Force, the Fountain, and all of these experiences have just being that, experiences appeared to teach me something and getting ready for the winer one.

I came to here, Lake Tahoe to wash the past, and clean myself with these blue waters and be grateful with the experiences I learned, why why why? There is no more. I accepted, I lived and now have to let it go. Universe has given me everything and now I feel the Universe in Me, Thank you, Thank yo, thank you, because this discerning wouldn't come if this journey wouldn't happen.

I learned that you can give love and be in love and its okay, but perhaps the other one don't want to give love, because they just don't know it. But the absence of love is pain and fear and understood I don't want to be around those, I only want to be and mingle with lovely people.

I don't think that's too much to ask. But hey feel free to drop your fears here and now and start experimenting the richness of Love.

Because there is certainly a future and your hope will not be cut off

Love wont fail, if it does wasn't love anymore, and what it ends to be never was